SWEETNESS IN NOSTALGIA

CHERISHING THE PAST AND LIVING THE PRESENT

T ABRAHAM

Contents

Contents

Contents

Credits

All the images used in this book are created with the help of the Artificial Intelligence technology available in the Canva.

Preface

Once we have lived in the past it is a rule by nature that one is living in the present and is going to see a future which can be interpreted to a certain extant but can never be determined completely. Interpretation and perception are something that can be done by us or namely by the human race or the created. The creator is our Almighty God and our heavenly father who sees us both intrinsically and extrinsically. Our thoughts determines our actions and our purity in heart and mind to some extant is visible to the human eyes. There are always sweet thoughts and innocent actions seen in every child and we too have passed this stage. So, here we are going ponder upon the sweetness shed to us by these memories which keeps on ringing inside one's mind.

It is universally accepted and experimentally not approved that one can travel back to one's past life and live in it and change the present and instantaneously the future. This is impossible because there has not been anyone so talented and knowledgeable enough to break the nature's order and to make one travel across times of past, present and future. There are cartoons that talk about time machines and time travel but, it is something against the order of nature and one has not yet broken it to make this happen yet.

Even though one cannot make a journey through physical means to one's past but we can travel through our minds by the memories that were created during our stay in that particular time. Many of us experience the memories ringing inside our minds and appearing as faint flashes yet very sweet to think upon. Nostalgia and nostalgic thoughts are something that are always very pleasing. Nostalgia is a feeling which is created by the sweetness of one's past which is urging one's mind to live in that particular time frame and gives one the feeling of longingness for it.

When we compare the traumatic experiences with these thoughts of sweetness it is always seen that both come to us at an equal rate but it is always a win-win situation for the goodness over the staleness and rottenness given to us through these experiences. Many of us wants to live in a carefree world of our childhood days or want to live during our adventurous or adventure seeking teenage. As we are tending towards the future we may loose many things as one needs to travel in the pathway of responsibilities and also one would loose the carefree attitude and a carefree world as one has to think and decide upon many things that can either sustain or destroy our comforts and happiness.

Hence, the sweetness can be felt by a travel to our pasts through our mind. And it is also very important for one to taste these sweetness of happiness sometimes to get away from the tiresome adulthood days and to boost oneself with energy and strength to get prepared towards a happy future.

T ABRAHAM

CHENNAI, 2024.

Acknowledgements

I would like to thank Dr S. Samuel Rufus sir for encouraging me to identify the dormant poet inside me. I would like to thank sir for constantly motivating me throughout the completion of the 50 poems and for reading the manuscript for finalizing it for publishing. I would also like to thank Dr Mekala Rajan ma'am, Former Head of the Department of English (Aided), Madras Christian College (Autonomous) for motivating me to start writing poems which made me pen down my first three poems which instantly got elevated and has resulted in completion of 150 poems in which my first 50 poems were published as a book titled 'I ADMIRE YOU - A SELF-ADMIRATION OF MY INNER FEELINGS' and my next set of 50 poems were published as a book titled 'Loud Inner Voice: Multiple voices ringing inside' and this book contains the poems written after the publication of my second book. I would like to thank Mr J. Arun Kumar sir for being a constant support throughout the writing of this book.

I would like to thank Dr. S. Franklin Daniel sir, Head of the Department and the Department of English (Aided), Madras Christian College (Autonomous) for equipping me with this wonderful art of writing poetry which has resulted in the creation of my third book titled 'Sweetness In Nostalgia'.

Last but not the least, I would like to thank my mother and my friends for being a constant support which made me complete writing this book within a limited time frame.

1. The Drops That Pause

The drops of the sky,
That pops from the clouds,
Drops to fill up the land,
Puddles to be careful about,
It makes me pause at times,
Pausing from my routine,
Pausing from the rush,
It pauses the vehicles,
It blocks my way,
Puddles to look about,
Land filled with mud,
My soles getting dipped,
I am about to trip,
But I do not want this,
Puddles everywhere to pause,
These drops make me pause,
I tell you, it makes me pause.

2. The Bubbling Pot

Bubbling in happiness and joy,
My heart is bubbling,
The cheerful and pure blood,
Fills up my limbs and soul,
The season has come here,
After a fortnight plus one,
It is bubbling everywhere,
Pots with milk, jaggery and rice,
Turmeric as it's spice,
The one which fights the germs,
Germs of sadness and gloom.
The year blooms with a lots of happiness,
The sweetness is shared everywhere,
People on their glamorous colours,
Strolling around everywhere,
It is the tradition they say,
It is a happiness today,
The pot bubbles with foam,
And with a joyous air,
They all went home.

3. Fooled by Fakeness

It is easy to fall prey,
Prey for rumours,
Fallen by fakeness,
Getting fooled by words,
It is not an April fool,
Fooled by the evil,
Blinded by the shadows,
The truth was hidden,
It was hidden under the curtains,
I could not see it,
Unable to see this truth,
But at last it was rising,
Just as the dawn comes,
Slowing the sun is rising,
The truth is rising,
Rising to bring light,
The whole situation is lightened,
All the gloom went away,
Now all the flowers started to bloom.

4. Something to Everything

My journey begins with something,
With something in my hands,
Something to sustain and some money,
With something in my mind,
My mind has some hope and faith.
Every journey is landing in between,
I am standing at the station,
A station called 'nothingness',
No hope, money nor faith,
But I stay humble to my Lord,
The Almighty is testing me,
My patience and my faith,
Something to nothing,
Every journey brings us here,
I am reaching my destiny,
The destiny where I get anything,
Where I am blessed with everything,
I am landed here,
From nothing to everything.

5. The Connecting Quarrel

The quarrel has started,
Not a violent quarrel,
But I was irritated by you,
You were innocent,
But I was angry,
Angry by your presence,
I wished you just perished,
I wish I did not meet you,
But days went by,
Months passed by,
I found something in you,
You found something in me,
Something was connecting us,
Not the similarities,
Not the differences as well,
But the intersection was,
The place where we met,
It's been a decade,
One good friend to remember,
It is you whom I met,
You are my only true friend.

6. The Gold and The Almighty

I was tempted by these metals once,
By the Gold and Silver,
These precious metals of earth,
But not so precious as my Lord,
It was catching my sight,
Took a few and stored it inside,
The anger of the Almighty was burning,
It was bringing misfortunes indeed,
The citizens were doubting,
I was caught red-handed,
Almighty burned me down,
With me and my possessions,
The misfortunes all went away,
Even I went away with the ashes,
My soul flied away like the blue birds.

7. The Uniqueness

I am not blind to follow something,
Not blindly following someone,
But many are blindly following me,
Blind followers indeed is a sign of something,
Followers indicate you are unique,
Your uniqueness leads you and guides many,
But turn back and ask them to quit,
It is my uniqueness and it's my own,
None can copy it nor paste it,
It is mine alone and for none to claim.

8. Interrogate and Introspect

Questions running crisscross,
Asked to know the known,
Questioned to think upon,
I am questioned to get convinced.
Is it truth or fake ?
Did they investigate ?
Fakeness covering up the truth,
Soon the germs will catch the tooth.
The whole mouth is foul,
Smelling foul and overflowing with lies.
A liar will burn up in fire,
Fire around them and fire everywhere,
These questions makes me introspect,
But what has happened is genuine,
Law is equal to all,
None above the line or below it,
But some tells they do not fall into it.
Is it justice or misuse ?
Misuse of power will cause the decay.
Introspection tells about the incident,
Genuineness is needed,
Whoever you be and wherever you are,
The truth is coming on it's way,
It is slow but steady,

It is not faded or hidden,
Coming right in front of you to strike,
Politics cannot hide it,
Nor your power cannot stop it,
It is travelling on it's own way,
It is coming one day,
I tell you again and again,
It will strike you hard one day.

9. Need or Want

Desire to become,
Waiting for something,
Desire to have it,
Waiting to move on,
Desires and wants are luxury,
Waiting and needs are essential,
The Almighty provides us,
Provides us with our needs,
Need to survive or live,
But not with the luxuries,
Materialistic luxuries kept unfulfilled,
Do you have a need or want ?
Want is not a need,
Need cannot be want,
So does the time goes on.

10. The Reward Taken

The burning fire burns everything,
Just as how the fire is strong,
So is the punishment from the above,
He who showers upon you things,
Would shower upon you the rewards,
It is his will to give you the reward,
But he who has taken it away,
Hidden the reward to be given,
As a gratitude to the almighty,
There stands as strong as the hill,
The burning fire on the hill,
Burning anger of God was filled,
Filled the whole village and town,
So up above the hill he went,
The thief of the offering finally found,
But the furious fire and anger,
Burnt him down and ashes around,
No sound of wailing, but joy around,
The wrath has passed away,
Blessings more to come around,
The place is blessed and so are the crowd.

11. Burning My Past

The past hurts,
How fast it went,
Poking my thoughts,
Piercing my veins,
The past still stays,
The insults and cries,
The bullies and fright,
The deception in life,
Deceive to win,
I am deceived by you,
The past writ on paper,
The past around the air,
It is bitter and bitter,
The bitterest truth of all,
But you are just a paper,
A paper writ to be burned,
I am burning the past agonies,
I am burning the trauma,
I am burning you to ashes,
Never more you appear in flashes.

12. I Accepted You

Acceptance is difficult,
In this world of deception,
Trust and truth hardly found,
The air is always foul,
But I was deceived by you,
Your authority was genuine,
But it was just deception,
I accepted you as a confidant,
I was fooled by you,
Misuse of power and authority,
I was caught amidst the storm,
The power dynamics complicate it,
The political power play was found,
I accepted you but you were a devil,
A serpent in my garden,
I thought you were harmless,
But you tried to bite me,
Here you go away from the way,
I have chopped you into pieces,
Never come back, nor turn back again.

13. A River Flowing Through My Palms

Rivers with crystal clear water,
Found on this earth with saltiness,
Rivers on the earth and land,
A river is flowing deep within my hands,
River on my soles and palms,
It drowns everything, wetting around,
Things may slip and fall around,
The papers are all wet around,
It is freezing and cold at times,
This sweat that comes abrupt many times,
Chemicals mix with this salty liquid,
Dust and dirt stick on to my palms,
The cloth is rolling on my palms,
To relieve this sweat from messing all around.

14. Rejection and Repulsion

I reject many things,
But accept only a few,
Not required to accept everything,
It does not mean to reject everything,
I reject the lust and dust,
Rejection of fakeness and falsehood,
I reject the evil and the suppressor,
With rejection comes the repulsion,
The ignorance is repulsive,
I repel and would not get attracted,
My sight is clean and pure,
Your sight is filled with lust and dirt,
I stand upon my decision,
I will follow the good and root out the other,
Never will I fall apart,
Never will I get amidst the wrong,
With rejection comes repulsion,
You are rejected and I repel,
Rejected the fake and ignorance takes it's way,
The rejection and repulsion is forever more.

15. A Dozen of Lies

Words of truth are less,
Lies are building up fresh,
The mouth of the social animal,
Less hospitable and sociable,
Less kind and more of lies,
Fakeness is building up,
Truthfulness is nowhere to be found,
It is hard to trust you,
No truth is building up,
Deceived under many situations,
Lies building like a heap,
A landfill for fakeness is built,
The river of truth is polluted,
With a dozen of lies as a polluter.

16. The Chatter Inside My Mind

Some sounds are heard,
Noises going out,
And voices coming in,
The noise or voice matters,
The voice is sensible,
It contains sense,
The noise is just a rattle,
With some non-sense,
The voice or noise,
That does not matter,
Voices of the past,
Noises of the last,
The overflowing voices,
With it's drowning noises,
Suppressing noises and voices,
Lasts only a little,
Optimistic voices and noises,
Chatter in my brain,
It chatters forever.

17. The Monosyllabic Power

The two letter word,
The word to reject,
This word is hard to say,
Or hardly ever uttered,
Is it easy to tell it ?
It is simple to tell,
Simplicity to reject,
This monosyllabic word,
'No' means 'no',
These two letters,
Easy to say but,
Difficult for many,
Just two letters,
These two letters,
Can save you,
Can protect you,
Two-letter word,
A word of rejection,
Reject the evil,
Walk to the light,
Light of God,
Tell N-O to the devil,
For temptations and fakeness,
This word is strong,

I tell you, 'No means no',
It does not tell anything else,
It does not mean 'wait',
Nor it tells, 'I will think',
The word uttered,
Is my first and final decision,
A decision of rejection,
No means 'no'.

18. The Battlefield

The open ground is everywhere,
Found anytime and everyday,
The ground for battles and duels,
Battles of shield and armor,
Fought on open field with swords.
The mind is a ground,
Ground of power play and misuse,
Battles of argument and accusations,
False claims and fakeness,
Fought anywhere with words,
Words of falseness and foolishness.
The kingdom is a space,
A space of wit and smartness,
Ground with marbles of whiteness,
A room filled with brightness,
The battle of wits takes place,
Battle with wisdom and knowledge.
Everywhere I see a battlefield,
Everyday I see this duel,
Life is a battlefield of everything,
A battlefield which is always moving.

19. The Innate Uniqueness

Everything changes with movement,
The time is changing,
The circumstances are changing,
The ambience is changing,
The atmosphere is changing.
Only some are constant,
Innate qualities are concrete,
Time tries hard and moves apart,
Innateness does not change,
Striving hard to be unique,
Innateness and uniqueness,
It charges the inner spirit,
Makes it more concrete with core,
The core innateness and values,
Never will it take a shorter path,
Nor will it try to ease itself,
The likeness to travel in a longer path,
The path with more permanence and truth,
The uniqueness never diminishes,
None can change it forever.

20. Influencing Ambience

The ambience with brightness,
My heart is pumping over,
The stream flows throughout,
My eyes open up with glitter,
My stomach has no sickness,
My muscles are stronger,
With a bright, constant and strong light.
The ambience is flickering,
My heart stops and struggles,
The stream is dried up,
My eyes are flickering,
My eyelids falls down,
My stomach is acidified,
Nauseating sickness ruling now,
My muscles are weak and loose,
With a dull, wavering and weak light.

21. The Blessed Land

Location of the past,
Destiny of the future,
Land of present wealth,
Blessed by the brilliant light.
Brown as the soil,
Golden as the oil,
Black as the pepper,
Redness of the chili,
Strong presence of turmeric,
Breeze by the coconut trees,
The Palmyra trees of sweetness,
Blessed black and brown races,
And faces of the world,
In the land of richness,
Dwelling in this beauty,
A beauty of nature,
Sculpted by the creator.

22. Oscillating Faces

One's opinion oscillates,

My view oscillates,

Oscillating from good to evil,

But never does the evil turn good,

From trust to fakeness,

But the fake not to trust,

The oscillator of life,

Taking me to and fro across,

A big path of life to cross,

Crossing the challenges,

Using a plenty of defences,

Many get offended,

The uniqueness is defended,

Once came a crowd,

Crowd of influencers,

Both positive and some proud,

Only one came forward,

Others moved backward,

The man came,

With a face to tame,

The already tamed one,

Tamed, untamed and retamed,

Polite, gentle and humble,

And not crumbled by none,

Hard to change,
And unmeasurable range,
The oscillating face,
An impossible case.

23. The Fading Fallacy

False claims and blames,
And truth burning by it's flames,
Truth flickering and fading,
But false judgements growing,
Hard for falseness to abstain,
But truth always would sustain,
It sustains till my last breath,
The truth never dies,
It is a universal truth,
A word of immortality,
The false is mortal,
The truth is immortal.

24. The Unleashing Swords

The mind as a whole,
Ideas on a bowl,
Stagnant they stay,
By time they fade away.
The box with a crack,
Light going to the rack,
Of pages and covers,
I sit under my room's bower.
The sword of insults,
The words of harm,
Cannot move the charm,
The results are seen,
For the time being,
The final results,
Passes the days unseen.
The sun rises,
The sword unleashes,
These insults and harm,
Brings out great results and charm,
The mind pours out,
Pouring out everything it has,
The brain is drained,
The papers are clogged,
Digitally the blog is clogged.

At this time of the year,
None nearby to hear,
But this screen,
A senseless screen near by,
Everything far by,
Bye and bye,
To all sensical things,
Things of the past,
Remains out of rust.
The things hidden,
Hidden long back,
Or left far back,
Waiting to meet,
Wanting to meet,
But these dull and eerie,
Coldness may pass by.
O thou great mind !
Heed by my side,
The living entity moves away,
The world falls apart,
But these swords unleash,
Unleash the words of pain,
Of words spoken of loss,
Waiting for brokenness to surpass,
The surpassing brokenness.
These negatives sharpen the sword,
The insults oiling the rust of it,
It broke my mind into halves,
The paper dipped in these halves.

25. Freshness and Contamination

Pleasant fragrance all around,
Flowering all over the ground,
The fragrance going in and out,
No evil nor any doubt.
The face with smile is true,
The smiling faces are false,
Few in number but true,
Available in plenitude and false,
False ruling over truth,
Truth lying underneath.
The days change into night,
The nights change into day.
One day or one night,
Day one or last night,
The smiling faces shrink,
Shrinks and frowns a lot,
From smile to frown they rot,
When none would have thought,
Darkest of times and years,
Brings in a lot of tears and fears,
The freshness contaminated,
The beauty in it's reality,

To reveal the true eternity.

26. The Raging Fire

Whenever packed up,
The whole potential filled up,
Competitive and fair,
Jealousy and unfair,
Surrounding all around the locale,
I heard the noises and chatter,
Calling the spirit to run faster,
Slow and steady,
But fast and ready,
To conquer your rights,
Safeguard your possession,
The raging fire has started,
As violently as the wind,
As terribly as the swirls,
Volcanic eruptions inside,
None to calm from outside,
The raging desires,
The ringing wishes,
Dreams to come true,
The desires are true.

27. The Dislike of Infringement

Interference in everything,

No freedom in anything,

Stop the infringement and interference,

Do not make a pattern alive,

I want all the shapes and shades,

Shapes and shades of life,

Shapes of success and failure,

Shades of all emotions,

Experience needed in growing,

Do not infringe and stop the growth,

No bower hinders me,

Nothing can cover me,

Waiting patiently for many,

Rushing things for none,

Stopping and waiting,

Rushing uncontrollably,

But do not infringe,

And never interfere.

28. Like Bones And Flesh

Like bones, it is my foundation,
Like flesh, it is my sensation.
Bones building my foundation,
Foundation in the essence,
Of writing and of speaking,
Of broadening and widening,
Expressive expression to be expressed.
Like flesh it is dressed,
Dressed upon this foundation,
Of thinking and of learning,
Of structuring and systematising,
Thinkable thoughts to be thought.
Words and thoughts are learned,
Thinking the thinkable,
Breaking past to think the unthinkable,
Words creating wonder and beauty,
And structure and systems doing its duty.
Truth and creation,
Both in their mutation,
Of words and thoughts,
Of books and book of books,
They are the bones and flesh.

29. The Disturbing Images

Some pleasing to eyes,
Pleasant and aromatic creation,
A smooth and flowery sensation,
Of the beauty of the world,
The dust in the creation,
Dust to make flesh and bone,
The man who is God's own,
The flowers and bowers,
Of nature's perfumed power.
Some piercing the eyes,
Of diseases and sickness,
The wrath burning in creation,
A rough and foul sensation,
Of ugliness and suffering,
The dust turning back to dust,
The place where it came from,
It is destined back to go,
It disturbs you and me,
The disturbance of images,
Continues for more ages.

30. Changing Seasons

The season of sunshine with its joy,
The invaluable dolls and toys,
Sunshine and sweat accompanied,
Smiles arising and secrecy accompanied,
Season concrete or changing ?
The clouds present in every season,
Unleashing the kindness to it's very reason.
The season of spring to cling,
Spring springs up with it's wing,
Flowers, fruits and fragrance,
Covering over the upcoming pestilence,
Season concrete or changing ?
The clouds crowding and glowing,
Unleashing the reason of this season.
The autumn bringing sickness,
Autumnal dampness and wickedness,
Falling apart and moving away,
The pestilence coming it's way,
Season concrete or changing ?
The clouds with their dampness raging,
The unleashed reason begins it's treason.
The wild winter rains raining,
The heart and blood frozen by moaning,
Wintery wildness and nothing pleasant,

Everything from the summer is present,
Changing seasons with their dark reasons,
Truth revealed by reasons received,
The smiles vanishing and the times changing.

31. Cloudless Skies

Skies with clouds and smoke,
Surrounding my locale with fog,
Clouds heavy and high above,
The place filled below with smog,
Clouds above and smog below,
The sun filled with it's yellow,
The mind with this fog clouded,
Makes the thoughts loaded,
The clouds and smoke are absent,
The thoughts with clarity is present,
The unknown hidden so long,
The long past which was written wrong,
The skies with no clouds,
There is not so many doubts,
The blues visible with magnificence,
The discovery made in innocence,
The truth discovered and unraveled,
The science of truth is found,
The wisdom and the knowledge differentiated,
When there is a clarity with brilliance,
The brilliant clarity present above.

32. The Perfect Dilemma

In anonymity, anxiety prevailing,
Anxious anxiety flowing,
The deadly death of anonymity,
The decaying denser thoughts pouring,
Flying, floating, flowing and pouring,
Waiting, wanting and watching,
Reddening redness like ruddiness,
Dilemma dining with time,
Perfection attained in dilemma,
Learning, leaning and standing,
The perfection in dilemma,
The perfect dilemma.

33. The Lost Essence

Sourness is said,
But cannot feel sour,
Sweetness is said,
Never tasted sweet,
Bitterness is told,
Cannot feel the bitter taste,
Salted with salt,
But cannot feel it at all,
Spiced with pepper,
But cannot feel the spice,
My taste buds are numb,
A numbness in my tongue,
The words uttered,
Heard and felt,
No essence is present,
Just mere words,
Mere sounds are heard,
It is lost forever,
The essence in the words,
Lost essence forever.

34. The Turning Wheels

The rotating rotations,
The revolving revolutions,
The earth in it's moving sphere,
The sounds that I cannot hear,
The fast motions of life,
The fast chopping knife,
From the day one,
Till this very day,
Many changes ranging,
From up above it's hanging,
Bouncing back and forth,
The unstoppable growth,
Growth in physicality,
The beauty and the eyes,
The new personality,
The wheels turned,
The rolling of the dice,
The progression and regression,
The realisation of unattainable,
No concrete things available,
Nothing is forever,
The wheels keep moving,
Everything and everyone in motion,
In this vast life on an ocean.

35. The Termination

36. The Long Breath

The air filling the filled,
The fear and nerves killing,
The long and weak fear,
The coldness hard to bear,
Over and over again,
Under the bower it came,
The place to rest,
The patience in test,
Testing patience and resting anger,
The fear in danger,
The longest breath ever,
One last time forever,
None to fear,
When the goodness is near,
The one long time,
And one last time,
The long breath of relief,
One strong belief.

37. The Pause For The Cause

None to find all around,
One and only way around,
The never ending circles,
Ongoing abundance through miracles,
The stops and jerks,
The workers and clerks,
The money in the purse,
All dried up for the worse,
The toil in the soil,
As lustreous as a foil,
None left in my pockets,
All launched like the rockets,
Their destiny to the markets,
The wealth untold,
But have a hold,
Pause and think,
Do not spend to blink,
Have a pause,
To save for your cause.

38. Hotness Of Anger

The rays are bright,
Vibrant bands striking,
The bands are breaking,
Striking and breaking with the light,
The anger with it's danger coming out,
The hotness in my temperament,
With no happiness and contentment,
The sunshine burning the peace,
And nothing to calm,
Not even the breeze.

39. Lost In The Past

The past life of restlessness,
Nights of sleeplessness,
The fruitful life becoming fruitless,
In the midst of progression,
There comes the regression,
The peace inside the mind,
Unable to find a place to bind,
Mindless, restless and fruitless,
The repeating and repeated history,
There prevails an unsolvable mystery,
The crimes of betrayal and fakeness,
The diminishing genuineness.

40. Drops Of Flavours

The sweet sweetness,
With the sugars and candies,
Sweetest honey from the nature,
Dropped inside the created creature,
The happiness filling the tongue,
Passing throughout the mouth,
The sweet words of kindness,
The sweetness in truthfulness,
An everlasting and unforgettable essence,
Power of the innocence.
The harsh bitterness,
Like the stings of the bees,
Buzzing all around in nature,
The pain in the sting,
Bitterness joining with a string,
The sadness and fear coming,
Anger and rudeness following,
No more of innocence,
It is lost forever with it's essence,
The poor and tampered innocence.
The needful salty presence,
The seas and oceans with it's essence,
Deception born for survival,
Goodness to kill the evil,

Fruitful overpowering the fruitless,
The fortunate rooting the misfortune,
To make one's life come to tune,
The saltiness of maturity,
Brokenness in innocence,
To make a powerful presence.
The everlasting morality,
With an immovable maturity.

41. Unshielded Element

The fears and tears of life,
Surrounding like a pointed knife,
No shield to protect,
Feared about evil contact,
The gloominess to fright,
The light shines bright,
The brightness in a muddle,
My fears drowned inside a puddle,
The storms with no norms,
None to protect with the shield,
No growth in the field,
The rust overpowering,
Sparkle no more sparkling,
The loss amidst the toss,
Nothing more than this loss.

42. Biased Disturbances

The law is blinded,
Sunshine and clouds,
No more sunrise,
The rise in the crowds,
The sun is ever set,
Unlawfulness and no faith,
Law with mere words,
No essence felt,
Authority is hidden,
The forbidden making an end,
In the way there comes a bend,
The bias drowned to death,
The sun ever shining,
Unbiased blessed with wealth.

43. Light Inside The Darkness

In darkness I see,
A truth like the sea,
The storms and winds,
Bringing out the quality,
Broken natured is the ship,
Crookedness innately present,
The crooked crowd,
Wickedness felt so loud,
In darkness one can see,
The brightness of the light,
The light of truth comes out,
The worst of times,
It is the best ever time,
The times of fakeness seized,
With the truth coming out unleashed,
Bitter truth being better,
Than the fake sweetness,
I cherish this bitterness,
This bitterness of the darkest truth.

44. Beyond The Line

Everything in some measure,
Gives one a healthy pleasure,
The lines controls it,
Boundaries drawn for it,
Sweetness in a drop,
Only a cup of sugar,
Else it is a flop,
More is often troublesome,
Plentitude is always troublesome,
Moving beyond the lines,
Infringement against the boundary,
The evilness invading the territory,
The context changing rapidly,
Self-dignity without innateness,
Troublesome intimacy of the devil,
Context changes from an authority,
The misuse leading to intimacy.

45. Undigestible Bitterness

Is it a reality or a dream ?
The inner reality in scream,
Truth hiding for a long time,
Coming out with it's bitterness,
Unacceptable and undigestible,
No enzymes are secreted,
A temporary pause,
Terrible shock as the cause,
Bitter betrayal seen everyday,
Seen everywhere and always,
Walking past in a thousand ways,
Bitterness filling all my days,
A harsh betrayal to hinder,
Fakeness is no wonder,
The falseness and fallenness,
The undigestible is surrounded,
Enzymes finally secreted,
The bitterness finally conquered.

46. Heresy In Innocence

The truth hard to follow,
Goodness unable to be tolerated,
Call for someone or somebody,
The truth and the sinless called,
Innocence is intolerable,
The very presence is unattainable,
Calling the truth as false,
Being saved by the innocence,
By his very presence,
For he is ever present,
The truth is ever pleasant,
Fakeness is followed,
An easy to follow business,
The impossible being away,
Saving many with sacrifice,
None to thank, but to stab,
False stabbing the truth,
The absence brings guiltiness,
The truth being ever present.

47. Diminishing Life

Fogginess surrounding,
Fakeness in the surrounding,
The glasses with the fog,
Trees turned to logs,
Big blocks by the logs,
Movement in stagnation,
Foulness surrounding everywhere,
The foulness in the evil,
Crimes smelling foul,
The nature, unpredictable,
The judgement is true,
Being judgmental, called rude,
Never been so rude,
The judgement at my first sight,
The first impression,
Stopped the fog of depression.

48. Near A Trap

A place of fantasy,
The place of total misery,
Mask of goodness,
The masked evilness,
No fantasy, nothing good,
The devil and misery,
Rattraps of the world,
Trapping the mind,
Intellect for crimes,
Misusing the trust,
Fakeness coming out,
Intentional crimes,
Nothing unintended to rhyme,
The trap is around,
Nothing can surround,
A crash to break,
No more innocence,
Never will I be present,
A more safe place,
Search for truth,
Nothing can trap me,
Nor am I trapped,
The search continues,
Finding comfort and peace,

Comfort in true fantasy,
A truth found in peace.

49. Revolving Pasts

Circles with no end,
A vicious circle should end,
No mark of origin,
None to mark the end,
The cycles of anger and pain,
Falling upon like an acid rain,
The rain with contamination,
A contaminated space of a nation,
History repeating it's pattern,
Events forming life pattern,
Bleeding without cotton,
The wound, unwound and exposed,
Now I am dead and rotten,
The past rotting and clotting,
Breath pausing and resuming,
Nearing the death bed,
Waking up in the life bed,
Time moving past,
Times of future to come,
Rottenness of mind and soul,
Still remains fresh,
For the days are more.

50. Drained Energy

Just mere flesh and blood,
No thoughts and no flood,
No more smiles and laughter,
More are the evilness around,
The evil unleashed to disturb,
A cheerful soul which lived once,
Innocent soul, so unique in nature.
But dead, it is forever now,
The body with it's flesh and blood,
A damage so well done,
Excellent performance by the evil,
Tampering and scratching the peace,
The body is now at no ease,
But it is mentally dis-eased.

I Admire You: A Self-admiration Of My Inner Feelings

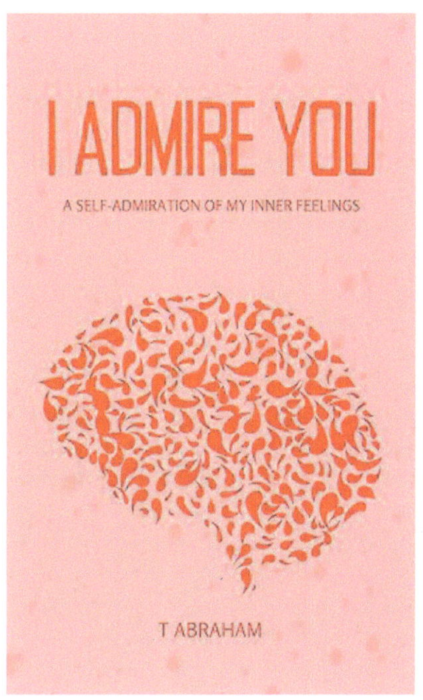

I Admire You is a collection of poetry which deals with feelings and emotions that reach the extremities. A life which gives you a spoonful of all the feelings in every stage of growing up is described. The feelings and emotions are weaved using words to create this collection of poetry. The title is given due to the self-admiration of my inner feelings.

Publisher: BookLeaf Publishing, Srinagar
ISBN: 9789358316506
Published on: November 13, 2023

Loud Inner Voice: Multiple Voices Ringing Inside

Loud Inner Voice is a collection of 50 poems that views the everyday life in a scrutinized manner. The poems are written from the varoius thoughts that rings in my mind to create a variety of voices.

Publisher: Notion Press, Chennai

ISBN: 9798893223248

Published on: March 7, 2024

www.ingramcontent.com/pod-product-compliance
Lightning Source LLC
Chambersburg PA
CBHW040852110726
48005CB00001B/30